The Rockwool Foundation Research Unit

Immigration and Welfare State Cash Benefits
– The Danish Case

Peder J. Pedersen

University Press of Southern Denmark
Odense 2011

Immigration and Welfare State Cash Benefits – The Danish Case

Study Paper No. 33

Published by:
© The Rockwool Foundation Research Unit and
University Press of Southern Denmark

Copying from this book is permitted only within
institutions that have agreements with CopyDan,
and only in accordance with the limitations laid
down in the agreement

Address:
The Rockwool Foundation Research Unit
Sølvgade 10
DK-1307 Copenhagen K

Telephone	+45 33 34 48 00
Fax	+45 33 34 48 99
E-mail	forskningsenheden@rff.dk
Home page	www.rff.dk
ISBN	978-87-90199-55-5
ISSN	0908-3979
May 2011	
Print run:	300
Printed by	Specialtrykkeriet Viborg
Price:	60.00 DKK, including 25% VAT

Contents

Abstract 5
1. Introduction... 7
2. The migration background 8
3. Indicators of labor market integration.................... 10
4. Benefit programs – status and changes since 2000......... 15
5. Survey of existing studies on welfare dependence 18
6. Development in welfare dependence since 2000 24
7. Conclusions... 34
References 36

Immigration and Welfare State Cash Benefits
– The Danish Case[*]

Peder J. Pedersen
School of Economics and Management, Aarhus University

Abstract

The purpose in this paper is to summarize existing evidence on welfare dependence among immigrants in Denmark and to supply new evidence with focus on the most recent years. Focus is on immigrants from non-western countries. The paper contains an overview of the background regarding immigration in recent decades followed by a survey of relevant benefit programmes in the Danish welfare state. Existing studies focus on both macro analyses of the overall impact from immigration on the public sector budget and on micro oriented studies with focus on specific welfare programs. Existing studies focus on the importance for welfare dependence of demographic variables, on the big variation between countries of origin and on the importance of cyclical factors at time of entry and during the first years in the new country. Evidence from the most recent years reinforce the importance of aggregate low unemployment in contrast to fairly small effects found from policy changes intending to influence the economic incentives between welfare and a job for immigrants.

---

[*] The empirical part of this study is built on a micro panel data set made available by the Rockwool Foundation Research Unit. I am grateful for the opportunity to work with these data and grateful also for competent research assistance from Katrine Pedersen and Chalotte Bøgesvang. Constructive comments from a referee are gratefully acknowledged.

JEL Classification : H 53, I 38, J 61
Keywords: Immigration, general welfare programs, effects of welfare programs

Coresponding author:
Peder J. Pedersen
School of Economics and Management
Bartholins Alle 10
Aarhus University
DK-8000 Aarhus C
Denmark
Email: ppedersen@econ.au.dk

1. Introduction

In 2008 around 70.000 individuals came to Denmark as immigrants, return migrants or refugees. The inflow was at a level corresponding to 1.3 per cent of the population. Close to 30.000 persons emigrated in 2008. These flows are as well known composed of groups and individuals with big differences in background and motives for their mobility. In 2008 the Danish economy peaked with unemployment down to 2 per cent of the labor force. The big majority of immigrants, about 50.000 came from the group of socalled western countries including Danes who returned home after a stay abroad[1]. About 20.000 emigrated to western countries in 2008, resulting in the biggest net inflow from this group of countries ever recorded.

While these flows are mainly job or education related, the focus in the present paper is on the flows to and from the the non-western countries. The 2008 numbers relative to this group of countries were about 20.000 entering and about 10.000 leaving the country resulting in a net increase in the stock of non-western immigrants of about 10.000 persons. While the flows to and from the western countries in recent years have been clear reflections of the cyclical situation, it is interesting that this seems to appear also in the flows to and from non-western countries, i.e. immigration picks up from 2005 and emigration goes down from 2006 – the first reduction in emigration to non-western countries recorded since 1980.

While cyclical factors thus seems to influence also the flows to and from non-western countries in the most recent years, the big majority of people from these countries arrived as tied movers or refugees without a job or an educational placement standing open.

The topic in the paper is the meeting of this quickly growing group of immigrants and their descendants with the benefit programs in the Danish welfare state. Their qualifications and background, relative to the state of the Danish labor market, has an impact on the entry to benefit programs, the duration of spells on benefits and – most importantly – on the exit from benefit programs to self provision through a job.

In the following, Section 2 gives a short background to the Danish situation regarding the development of immigration. Section 3 summarizes indicators of

---

1 The main division regarding countries of origin used by Statistics Denmark is between
- Western countries consisting of the EU member states, Nordic countries outside the EU, Switzerland, Andorra, Liechtenstein, Monaco, San Marino, the Vatican State, Canada, USA, Australia and New Zealand
- Non-Western countries: Rest of the World

the labor market integration for non-western immigrants as having a job – or your own business – not surprisingly is a main factor for the present topic of benefit dependence or self provision. Section 4 summarizes the main components of the public sector cash benefit programs, including changes, mainly in relation to immigrants, which have been enacted since 2000. These changes represent a new element in the Danish welfare state, i.e. a move away from a universalistic principle where the same eligibility rules applied to all with legal residence. Identification of the impact from these changes has been difficult as they occurred at the same time as changes in immigration policy and in the cyclical situation.

Attempts to identify the impact from these policy changes are among the topics in Section 5 containing a brief survey of existing studies of the interaction between migration, benefit programs and the labor market in Denmark. Next, Section 6 presents some new contributions to the main topic of benefit dependence and labor market integration for non-western immigrants. The focus is on the years since 2000 as many of the existing studies focus on earlier years that differ regarding the inflow of immigrants, the immigration policy and the cyclical situation in the Danish economy. Finally, Section 7 concludes the paper.

2. The migration background

In Denmark immigration at a larger scale picked up in the 1960s and early 1970s when guest workers were actively recruited mainly from Turkey, Yugoslavia and Pakistan in a setting with excess demand for labour. The big cyclical turning point occurring in 1973/74 resulted in a stop to further guest worker immigration. At the same time Denmark entered the EU implying free labor mobility relative to other member states, as in the common Nordic labor market which had been fully realized since 1954. The mobility relative to other EU countries as well as the mobility to the other Nordic countries remained however at a fairly low level, characterized further by high levels of return migration.

While the oil price shock as mentioned was accompanied by a stop to further immigration of guest workers, those already resident in the country were allowed to stay and to bring family members as tied movers. In the years after 1973/74 tied movers were the main source underlying the increase in the stock of immigrants. From the mid-1980s refugees also arrived in increasing numbers, resulting in the same fundamental shift in the composition of immigrants as in many other European countries, i.e. immigrants and refugees from less developed, or non-western, countries became the clear majority in the aggregate stock of immigrants and descendants.

Until the mid-1990s this occurred in Denmark against a cyclical background with high unemployment in a labor market with a relatively high minimum wage, and increasing emphasis on linguistic and professional abilities in the current jobs, while the "old industrial" jobs were phased out. As a consequence of these factors, participation rates were low and unemployment rates were high among immigrants from less developed or non-western group of countries. From the mid-1990s the labor market situation improved quickly. At the same time, in 1999, a new and more focused law on integration was enacted, followed in 2002 by restrictions regarding tied movers and refugees as described further in Section 4. The combined effects of a strong increase in the demand for labor and policy changes have been increases in participation rates and decreases in unemployment among non-western immigrants as described in more detail in Section 3.

The actual development in the number of non-western immigrants since 1980 is shown in Figure 1. Over the nearly 30 years there is a five fold increase in the stock of immigrants and refugees along with an even stronger increase in relative terms in the number of descendants. As in other European countries the descendants represent a big and very important challenge regarding entry to the labor market and improving the educational situation.

Figure 1. Number of immigrants and descendants from non-western countries, 1980 – 2008.

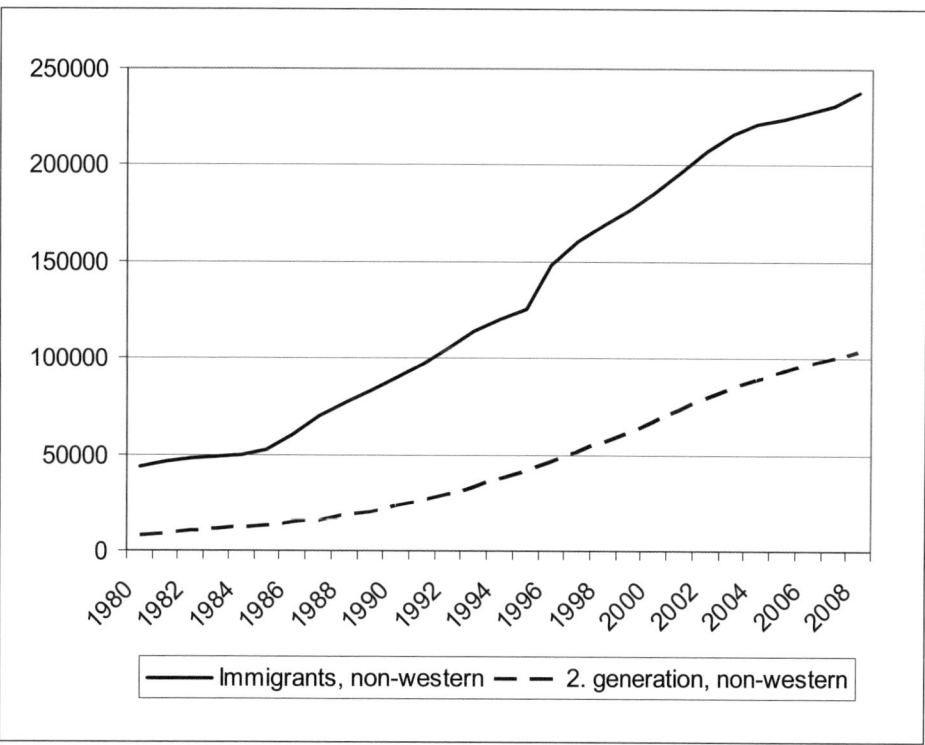

Next, Figure 2 shows how the stock shown in Figure 1 develops as the result of the annual net immigration from non-western countries. Except for the very last years, the migration flows are unrelated to the cyclical situation in the Danish economy. To a much higher degree they reflect variations in flows of refugees, most dramatically in the inflow of refugees from Bosnia in the mid-1990s.

Figure 2. Immigration and emigration, non-western countries, 1980 – 2008.

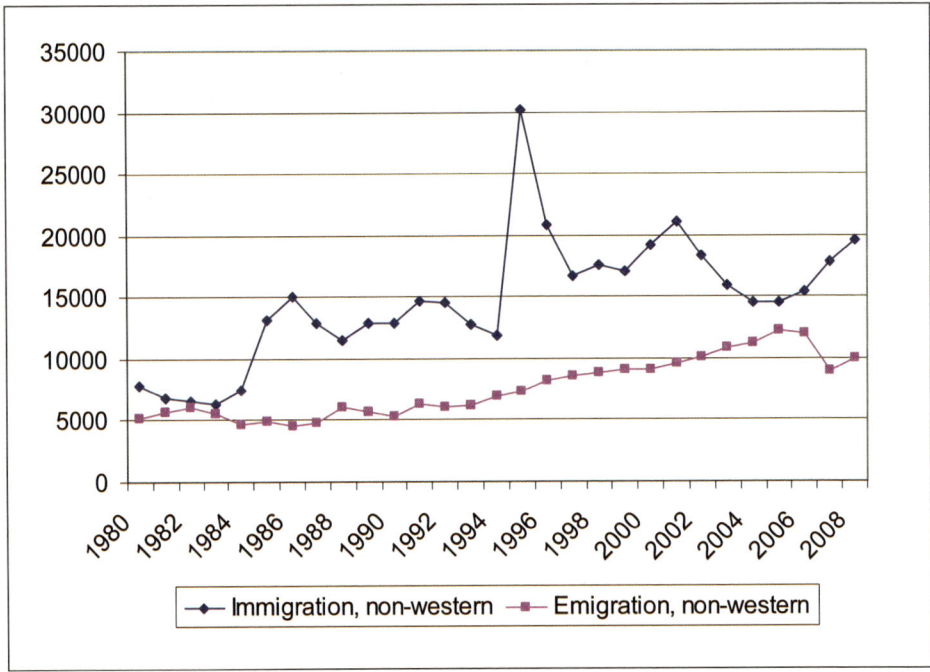

3. Indicators of labor market integration

Entering the labor market to get a job or open a business is a primary factor resulting in self provision instead of being dependent on cash benefits or being provided for by your family. It is obvious that important indicators in this area are the rate of labor force participation and the rate of employment conditional on being in the labor market. Figure 3 shows the overall participation rate for non-western immigrants for the most recent 10 years with available data. For comparison, Figure 3 also includes the participation rate for natives. For both groups the figure covers the age group 20 – 59 years old.

While native labor force participation has been nearly stationary since 1997, this is obviously not the case for non-western immigrants. Participation goes up with nearly 15 percentage points, most strongly in the cyclical upswing in the most recent years up to 2008.

Figure 3. Participation rates, Non-western immigrants and natives, 1997 – 2008.

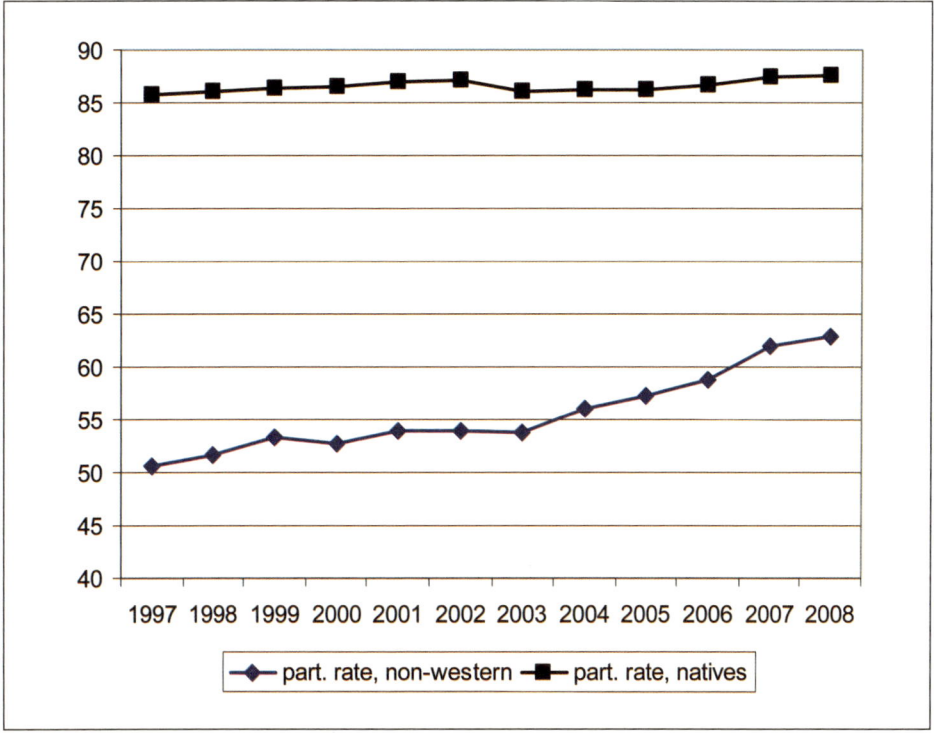

Two comments are necessary relative to Figure 3. Firstly, there is a big variation by national background around the overall immigrant participation rate. For people coming from the "old" guest worker nations the participation rates are stable, increasing slightly with the cyclical upturn while volatility over time is higher for newer arrivals. Secondly, the participation profile is looking much less like a success if a longer period from 1980 is included in the graph. Average participation for the whole group was 76 per cent back in 1980, i.e. higher than in the cyclical peak year of 2008. This long run profile is however affected by two big declines, reflecting not fundamental changes in the labour market integration, but instead the impact from two big waves of refugees arriving, cf. Figure 2, respectively 1985 – 1987 and 1994 – 1997. On each of these occasions, the summary average participation rate went down with 10 percentage points. The steady increase in participation from 1997 is not affected by such big exogeneous changes in arrivals but reflects instead a genuine improvement relative to the labor market.

Still, Figure 3 reveals an impressive 25 percentage points gap in participation rates between natives and non-western immigrants in 2008. In Figure 4 this is disaggregated by gender and age groups, showing a fairly small difference for young men, a much bigger difference in participation between men and women for non-western immigrants, in strong contrast to the situation for natives, and finally a much stronger decline in participation by age for the non-western immigrant group beginning already from about age 40. As a reflection of these profiles, the incidence of permanent benefits like disability pension is significantly higher among middle-aged non-western immigrants.

Figure 4. Participation rate by age. 2008.

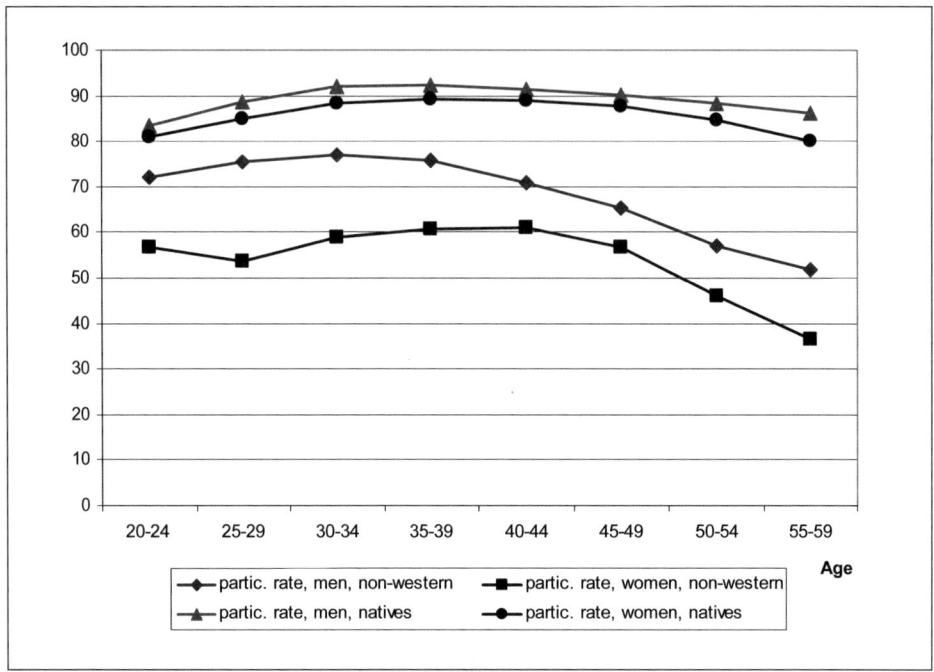

The significant increase in the participation rate for non-western immigrants shown in Figure 3 has a counterpart in employment rates. This is shown in Figures 5 and 6 disaggregating the change in employment rates by age and gender for non-western immigrants and natives between 2001 and 2008. The other side of the employment change over time is changes in dependence on non-permanent benefits, unemployment insurance and welfare assistance, to which we return in Section 6.

Figure 5. Change in employment rate for non-western immigrant women and native women between 2008 and 2001.

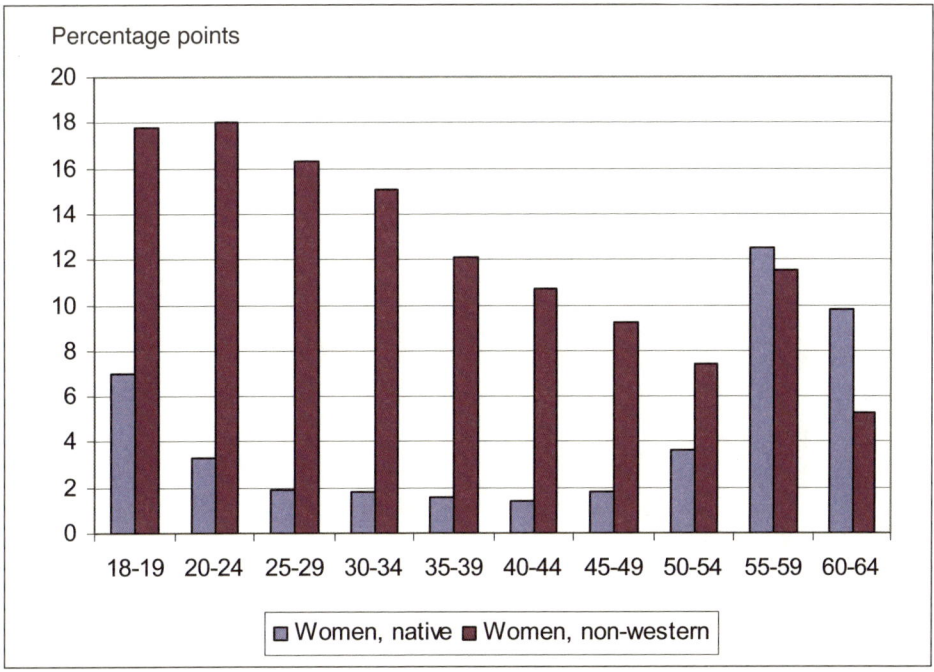

Figure 5 shows the quite impressive increases in employment shares for female non-western immigrants from 2001 to 2008. The increases are as seen strongly age dependent with 15 – 18 percentage points increases for those younger than 34. The surprising pattern for the 60 – 64 years old and even more so for the 55 – 59 years old is a reflection of a temporary early retirement program open for 50 – 59 years old individuals with more than 12 months unemployment (out of most recent 15 months) from 1992/94 until entry to the program was terminated in 1996. The development for immigrant women is benchmarked against the corresponding change for native women. The impact from the cyclical upswing is evidently much weaker for native women than for immigrants. For the 55 – 59 years old the big change in the employment rate for both groups of women reflects the program for early retirement which was closed to new entry from 1996.

Figure 6 shows the same pattern for non-western male immigrants, here with an even stronger reflection of the temporary early retirement program open for entry between 1992 and 1996.

Figure 6. Change in employment rate for non-western immigrant men and native men between 2008 and 2001.

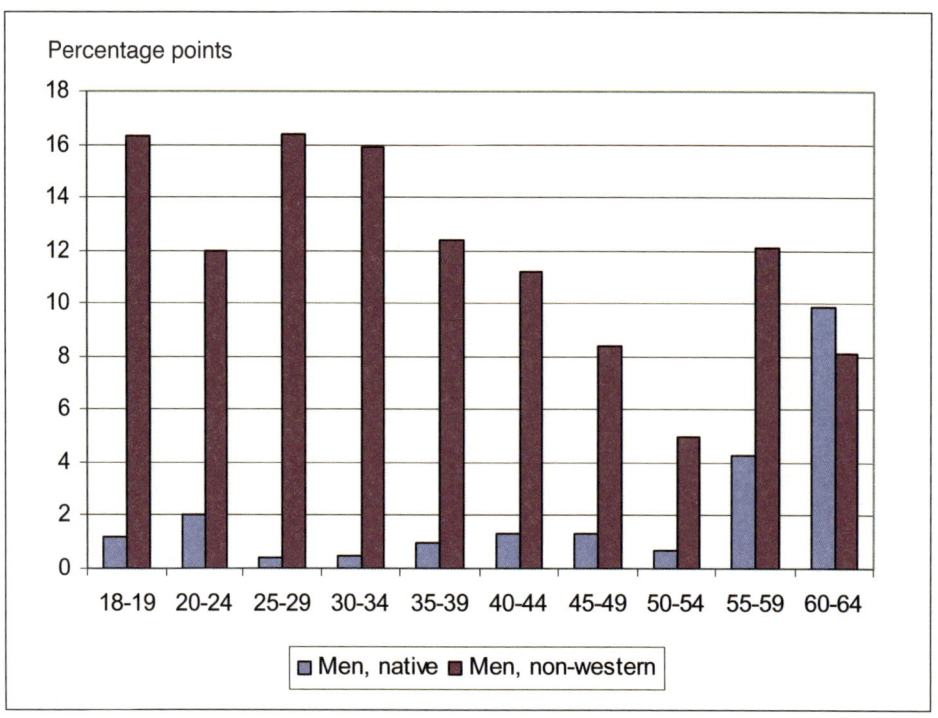

A final indicator of obvious relevance regarding benefit dependence is shown in Figure 7. The overall unemployment rate for non-western immigrants and descendants from 1996 to 2007 shows a dramatic decline from a level of 30 per cent down to 10 per cent in 2007. Compared with overall national unemployment in 2007 of 2,6 per cent the level for the immigrant group is still high. However, the decline is strong and reflecting a trend more than just a cyclical reaction and the gap between native and immigrant unemployment is lower in Denmark than in neighboring Germany and Sweden. For the young, 16 – 24 years old, Figure 7 shows the same strong decline in unemployment from 20 per cent in 1996 to 5 per cent in 2007.

Available quarterly data for full time unemployed non-western immigrants and natives from the first quarter of 2008 to the third quarter of 2009 shows an increase of 25 per cent for the non-western immigrants against an increase of 63 per cent for natives[2]. At least, as far as data are available for the period affected by the

---

2 These quarterly data are not fully comparable with the data behind Figure 7.

current crisis, immigrants seem to be less affected than natives by the economic crisis[3].

Figure 7. Unemployment rate, all and 16 – 24 years old non-western immigrants and descendants, 1996 – 2007.

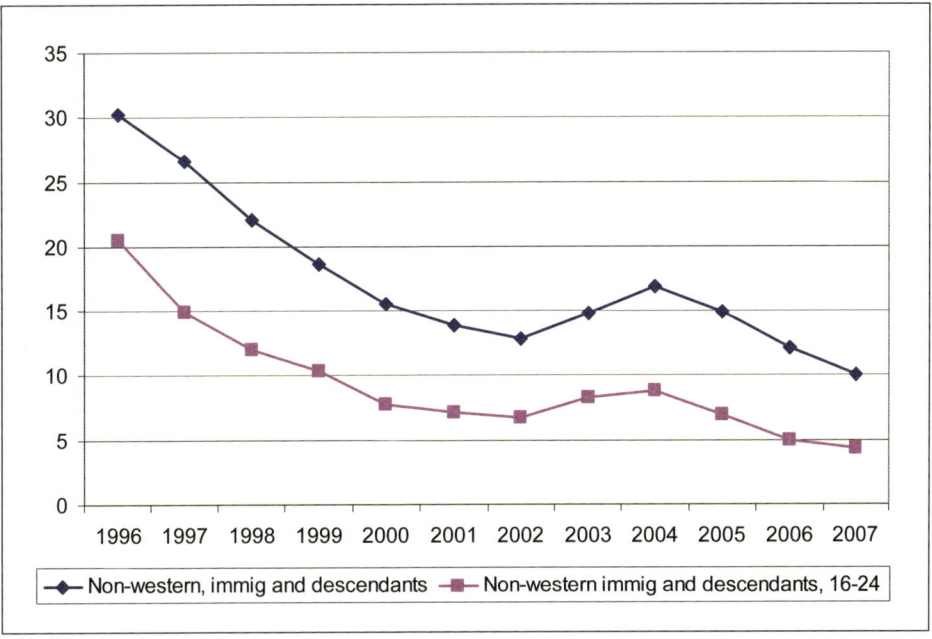

4. Benefit programs – status and changes since 2000

This section contains a brief survey of welfare state cash benefit programs in Denmark with focus on the years since 2000. The focus – also in Section 6 below – is on the non-permanent programs like unemployment insurance (UI) and Social Assistance (SA). National Old Age pension (OAP) and Social Disability Pension (SDP) on the other hand are quite dominatingly absorbing states or programs in the sense that individuals who enter these programs very seldom return to a job.

---

[3] This somewhat surprising fact could obviously reflect other factors than labor market integration, like differences by sector and differences in the age distribution. As one example, the current crisis has been especially severe in building and construction where fairly few non-western immigrants have been employed.

OAP consists of two components, a basic part to which nearly everybody 65 years and older are eligible and a supplementary part that is means tested. In principle, eligibility also depends on the fraction of time over the preceding 40 years people have spent in Denmark (but not conditional on what part of this period has been spent in the labor force). However, exceptions are used for immigrants who have been in the country for a shorter period. Furthermore, only a fairly small group of immigrants are older than 64. SDP – formerly a more narrowly defined disability pension – is granted on medical or social criteria. This is a permanent benefit program from which recipients are transferred to OAP when they reach age 65. The share of non-western immigrants receiving SDP is fairly low compared with natives, i.e. Nielsen (2002) found 4,4 per cent receiving SDP compared with 7,6 per cent of the natives. This, however, is influenced by differences in the age distribution. In a standard calculation correcting for age differences the non-western share receiving SDP was 10,5 per cent.

Two other permanent programs – or absorbing states in the sense that return from these programs to the labor force was, respectively is, very low – are a Transitional Benefit Program (TBP) and a voluntary early retirement program called the Post Employment Wage (PEW). The TBP was briefly mentioned above. From 1992 to 1994 eligibility to the TBP program – with benefits at 82 per cent of maximum unemployment insurance benefits – was conditional on 12 months of unemployment out of the most recent 15 months and being 55 – 59 years old. From 1994 – 1996 the eligible group was extended to include long-term unemployed 50 – 54 years old. Those covered by the program were transferred to PEW, cf. below, from age 60 and to OAP at age 67/65. Entry to the program was stopped in 1996, but with the youngest new entrant being 50 in 1996, a number of people were receiving TBP benefits until 2006. This program was used with a higher propensity by non-western immigrants than by natives.

The PEW program was created in 1979 as an early retirement option open for members of UI funds from age 60 without any health or long term unemployment criteria. This program has been used with a higher propensity by natives as a fairly small share of non-western immigrants are 60 and older and as a smaller share among them fulfilled the eligibility criteria based on duration of UI fund membership.

Focus in the present paper is as mentioned on the non-permanent programs characterized by a high propensity to return to or enter into the labor force. The two main programs are UI and SA. In Denmark UI is voluntary but the coverage is high. UI is organized in funds run in a certain cooperation with unions. Eligibility is depending on employment record and on fulfilling criteria regarding active job search and job availability. Benefits are 90 per cent of former earnings, but with an absolute ceiling implying an average rate of compensation around 60 per cent. A specific feature of the Danish UI system is that it is not means-tested and that the maximum duration since 1999 has been 4 years which is long in a cross-country context. In 2010, maximum duration was reduced to 2 years for unemployment spells beginning after July 1.

SA is available both for persons not covered by UI and with unemployment being their only problem and for persons with social problems beyond unemployment. Benefits are lower than UI and are means-tested. They are intended to be of limited duration, but are in principle (and in many cases in practice) of indefinite duration.

In 1998 Parliament enacted the socalled Integration Law creating a new legal base concerning immigrants and refugees. Labor market integration is the main explicit objective to be achieved by a combined effort involving mandatory language courses, education, labor market programmes, and by creating a higher priority regarding the challenge in local communities through a change in the administrative responsibility towards municipalities, away from the state and county administrations. The background for the new law was the cyclical upswing beginning in 1994 which created a much better environment than in the years from the mid-1980s to the mid-1990s when big numbers of refugees and immigrants arrived in a setting of a deep recession of long duration. In 2002 new laws were enacted creating a more restrictive immigration policy regarding granting permission of residence to refugees and regarding tied movers, especially in relation to marriage among people younger than 25 years.

Policy changes have also been implemented regarding cash benefits. In 1998 the socalled Introductory Benefits were implemented at a lower level than standard SA benefits. They were however soon increased back to the standard welfare benefits level. In 2002 the socalled Start Help program was introduced which at a level 35 % lower than standard SA benefits were intended for people who have not been residents in Denmark for at least 7 out of the most recent 8 years, i.e. discrimination against immigrants was avoided as the new rules also applies to a number of returning Danes. In analytical terms, the introduction of a new benefit level as of July 1, 2002 represents a "natural experiment" with regard to studies of the eventual impact from changes in economic incentives.

Another benefit related policy change is the introduction in the beginning of 2004 of a maximum ceiling of how much recipients of welfare benefits can collect in total of SA benefits, housing subsidies and specific support effective after receiving benefits for 6 months. When the ceiling is reached housing and specific benefits are reduced while the standard level of SA continues. The focus is not explicitly on immigrants, but in practice it turned out that a great majority of those affected by the policy change were immigrants. In a survey based study from 2005, Graversen and Tinggaard (2005) found no significant effect from the policy change on job finding. A final policy change enacted in 2006 was the introduction of an implicit maximum duration of SA to both partners in a marriage formulated as a demand for a minimum number of hours of paid work over a 2 years period. It is called the "300 hours rule" and is discussed further in Section 5.

The changes in immigration policy and in benefit programs, especially the changes regarding SA, occurred nearly simultaneously. They seem to have interacted in a number of ways reducing welfare dependence. The composition of new immigrants by age changed as a consequence of parts of the new immigration policy resulting in a higher average age for new entrants. The number of refugees applying for asylum went down strongly after 2001. Further, new immigrants coming as tied movers were not eligible for SA as they had to be provided for by their family as a condition for entry. The combined effect of the interaction between changes in immigration and welfare policies was thus an expected decline in the dependence on SA.

In the next section we summarize a number of studies of welfare dependence in Denmark with main emphasis on the post - 2000 years before presenting a new empirical material in Section 6.

5. Survey of existing studies on welfare dependence

The problem of welfare dependence can be addressed in different ways. Most broadly, some studies approach it by adding up the impact – in accounting terms – from immigration on public sector revenues and expenditures[4]. Other studies focus on dependence on specific benefit programs and study the incidence of entry to a program and the duration of spells on a specific program for immigrants typically benchmarking against natives. This section contains a brief survey of the broad approach followed by a survey of more program specific studies with main emphasis on studies after 2000.

The Danish welfare state has at least until recently been of the universalistic type, i.e. eligibility rules to most benefit programs have been the same for all with legal residence in the country. This fact has in a number of studies using the broad approach led to Borjas' idea of "welfare magnets" (Borjas, 1999) being one of the starting points. The idea here is that the choice of a host country is influenced by eligibility to and generosity of welfare programs. A competing theory is that networks of already resident groups of immigrants is a major factor behind arrival patterns for new immigrants. This, in combination with immigration policies,

---

4 The expression accounting terms is used to indicate that this type of exercises do not include the eventual impact on wages, prices and native employment.

implies that simple predictions from the "welfare magnet" theory are not verified in broad empirical analyses, cf. Pedersen et al. (2008).

A broad survey of studies from a number of countries, including Denmark, is found in Barrett and McCarthy (2008). Among the main conclusions are
- Unclear results regarding the "welfare magnet" theory
- Finding of very different results between countries with respect to where immigrants are using welfare programs more intensively than natives.

Nannestad (2004) raises the broad question of whether immigration – with focus on non-western immigrants – is a solution to the problem of ageing of the Danish population or whether it is a challenge for the Danish welfare state. The conclusion in Nannestad (2004) is that so far non-western immigration has had a negative net impact on the fiscal balance in the Danish welfare state. The conclusion is supported by results in Wadensjö and Orrje (2002) from calculations of the net fiscal impact of immigration and by a number of more general arguments. The main arguments here combines the weakening of economic incentives due to redistributive welfare programs with a labor market with entry barriers in the form of a relatively high minimum wage and a language problem. Nannestad (2007) is a broad survey of 15 years of research into the interaction between immigration and the welfare state. Nannestad (2007) concludes his survey of the impact from pull factors, from immigrant behavior after entry to the host country and the impact from immigration on the economy and welfare system in the host country by emphasizing
- A risk of erosion of the political support of the welfare state
- That excess unemployment of foreign born is highest in the Scandinavian universalistic type of welfare states
- That eventual policy reforms/changes depend on conclusions regarding the relative importance of selection against moral hazard, i.e. whether the reforms should target immigration policy or welfare reforms

Pedersen (2000) uses panel data for the period 1984 – 1998, i.e. including the last year before the changes in integration and immigration policies. This is the period with a strong, volatile increase in non-western immigration, cf. Figure 2. At the same time it is a period with big shifts in the distribution between tied movers and refugees and in the composition on countries of origin. Pedersen (2000) finds
- Big differences in the dependence on non-permanent benefits between countries of origin
- For 1998 he finds that non-western immigrants take up nearly 40 per cent of SA while being only 5 per cent of the population
- Also for 1998 a probit analysis of receipt or not of SA shows significant results for gender, country of origin, immigration year, language qualifications, education and an inverted U-shape in age

- For the period 1984 – 1998 he finds a stronger cyclical sensitivity for immigrants than for natives.

Nielsen (2001) analyses the eventual impact from benefit programs from the supply side by quantifying the share of natives and non-western immigrants (and descendants) with a gap less than 500 DKK (70 euro) monthly between disposable earnings in a job and benefits in case of unemployment. For non-western female immigrants and descendants 1998/99 calculations result in about 30 per cent of the immigrant group having less than 500 DKK as the gap between earnings and benefits – both calculated after tax. There is a risk that a gap that small /(and for part of the 30 per cent being even negative) can have an impact on job search and welfare dependence.

Nielsen (2002) is using panel data for the years 1985 – 2000. Welfare dependence is found to be a duration effect more than a result of a higher entry rate to welfare than found for natives. In a specific analysis of duration, focusing broadly on SA or being in activation or rehabilitation for 4 out of the 5 years 1996 – 2000, Nielsen (2002) finds a low incidence of 4 years duration for people from the "old" guest worker countries, but a high incidence for immigrants (tied movers and refugees) from Iran, Lebanon and Somalia. For the whole period 1985 – 2000, Nielsen (2002) finds an inverted U-shape over time for the share of immigrants being provided 80 – 100 per cent for by one of the different welfare programs. This time profile is a complex outcome from big changes in the cyclical situation in combination with big variation in the composition on countries of origin. Finally, Nielsen (2002) in a probit analysis of receiving SA or not in 2002 finds expected impacts from demographic variables and from years since migration. The quite dominant impact is – as expected – from the degree of attachment to the labor force.

In Rasmussen (2004) focus is on economic incentives in the choice between different welfare programs and between these and taking a job. The programs included are SDP, PEW, UI and the alternative is employment in a job. The job interface is with UI as the two other programs as mentioned earlier are close to be absorbing states. The study uses panel data for the period 1992 – 1998, i.e. including the peak unemployment years 1992-1993 and the first part of the subsequent cyclical upswing. Rasmussen (2004) estimates a random coefficients model to account for unobserved heterogeneity and finds significant impact on individual transitions from economic incentives both regarding transitions between welfare programs and between UI and a job.

Rosdahl (2006) presents results regarding the chances for acquiring a non-temporary job for a sample of non-western immigrants who initially are covered by one of the non-permanent benefit programs. The sample is fairly small but combines survey information with data from administrative registers. The data are collected in 2004/2005. Most of the factors found to be significant for the – fairly small – probability of getting a non-temporary job were as expected, i.e. experience, also in the home country, Danish language qualifications, self assessed health and the local labour market situation. It is interesting that no significant impact was found from assumed economic incentives on the probability of employment.

Blume and Verner (2007) study explicitly the welfare dependence by setting up a welfare dependence rate defined as the ratio between the sum of all public income transfers and the total individual income. The study uses panel data for the period 1984 – 1999. Tobit regressions are performed on the welfare dependence ratio separately for natives and immigrants and by gender. Beyond standard demographic variables, the explanatory variables include years since migration, age at migration, lagged individual unemployment and the aggregate unemployment in Denmark in the year of arrival.

The results are as expected regarding the standard demographic variables including education. Aggregate unemployment at time of entry is significant but the effect is very small. It is, however, surprising that this "scar effect" is most pronounced for western immigrants. Concerning the main question of whether immigrants assimilate out of or into welfare benefits the results are mixed. For this period, it turns out that non-western immigrants assimilate out of welfare looking at the period up to 20 years after entry. However, after about 20 years of residence the process reverses as non-western immigrants now assimilate into welfare programs. This reflects an age dependent shift in the relative importance of welfare programs from non-permanent to permanent or "absorbing" programs. Overall, the net effect is that immigrants for the period under study assimilate out of welfare benefits but the welfare dependence rate stabilizes at a relatively high level after 15 – 25 years.

Deding and Jakobsen (2008) are using a sample collected in 2006 combining survey and register data to study the eventual impact from attitude variables in explaining the gap in employment rates between native women and female immigrants 18 – 45 years old coming from Iran, Pakistan and Turkey. Responses to 12 survey questions are used to construct 3 attitude indicators on respectively gender roles, receipt of benefits and religion. In the present context, the attitude indicator regarding benefits is the most relevant. Deding and Jakobsen (2008) find a significant impact on the probability of being in a job from the benefit indicator but only for native women, i.e. only native women have a higher probability of being in a job, the higher is the wage relative to being on benefits. This is in contrast to the impact from attitudes towards gender roles which is only significant for immigrant women.

A general survey of the integration process and integration policy, including the recent changes in the form of eligibility only to reduced SA in the first 7 years of residence and a minimum demand on the number of hours with paid work for married people over the preceding 2 years to remain eligible for SA, i.e. an implicit way of introducing a duration limit on SA, is found in Economic Council (2007). This report also contains the results from a duration model of the probability for tied movers of getting a job during the first 2 years of residence in Denmark. Expected results are found for demographic variables and significant results are found also for a regional variable and a cyclical indicator. As individuals coming as tied movers must be provided for by their family or by getting a job as they are not eligible for public benefits, the analysis is less relevant in the present context.

As mentioned in Section 4 a new Integration Act came into effect in 1999. A first general assessment of the 3 years introductory program contained in the Integration Act can be found in Clausen et al. (2006). The data coverage is up to 2003 and as the introductory program has a duration of 3 years it is no surprise that lock-in effects are still very important regarding the probabilities of getting a job or becoming self provided. Job training in private firms appears (as usual) as the most successful instrument, but it should be kept in mind that other instruments, e.g. language education, has a potential long run positive impact which, for the lack of a sufficiently long observation period, is not captured here. It is interesting to note that self provision in about half the cases is due to the person being provided for by a spouse, and not by getting an ordinary job.

In a more recent study on time until regular employment for new immigrants Clausen et al. (2009) use micro data to analyse the impact from participation in labor market programs and in language training. They find a substantial "lock-in" effect from participation in active labor market programs as in the 2006 study, cf. above. The post-program transition to employment is affected significantly and positively only from wage subsidy programs. Regarding the eventual impact from courses improving the language proficiency of newly arrived immigrants, they find a significant and substantial positive impact on the transition to a job.

One of the specific policy changes described in Section 4 was the introduction of the programme called Start Help consisting of a reduction of SA to 65 per cent of the normal level for the first 7 years spent in the country. The explicit purpose was to change incentives making job entry more probable. The first analysis of the impact from Start Help, Hansen and Hansen (2004) studying the very first period of the new set up, found very low effects of Start Help. The Ministry of Employment (2005) in a study covering a somewhat longer period found a positive impact on job finding. Danish Employers Association (2006) has a positive – descriptively based – evaluation, but points out that some of the positive developments in the employment of new immigrants and refugees up to 2006 also must be seen in relation to the decrease in entry (and the improved cyclical situation). Rosholm and Vejlin (2007) in an econometric analysis find a small positive effect on the job finding rate but also a positive effect on the rate of exit from the labour force. As a consequence the overall net impact on employment is an empirical question. In a recent study, Huynh et al. (2007) compare the employment share after 16 months of residence for all refugees arriving in the 12 months before and the 12 months after the policy change in the middle of 2002. Huynh et al. (2007) find an impact, although fairly small, as 14 percent of the post-policy change group are employed compared with 9 percent of the pre-policy group. The analysis is continued in Huynh et al. (2010) finding – depending on specifications – that the employment effect is in the interval 3,3 – 6,2 percentage points. This corresponds to fairly high labour supply elasticities but the initial employment level is low. A side effect of the policy change is a considerable reduction in income for those who do not become employed.

Another tightening of SA was the introduction in the beginning of 2006 of a socalled "300 hours rule". This implied that married couples where both receive SA must have at least 300 hours of work each over a 2 years period. In case this is not fulfilled, SA is stopped for one of the spouses.. Persons with no or very little work capacity are exempted from this. From mid 2011 the rule will be 450 hours of work for each partner over a 2 years period. Bach and Larsen (2008) have studied the impact from this change in benefit rules on the labour market behaviour for the affected individuals. The study is based on register data as of September 2007 and interviews up to January 2008 of a sample under risk consisting of individuals loosing SA in 2007 or being under risk for this occurrence. In this group more than 90 per cent are born abroad. Bach and Larsen (2008) find an impact on employment as 33 per cent of those who lost their SA were in employment at the time of the interview while nearly the same share, 34 per cent became provided for by their family. Like Start Help and the SA ceiling rule, a side effect is that a considerable share of those affected by the policy change experiences a significant decline in income.

The three SA tightenings enacted since the beginning of 2004 have had an impact mainly on immigrants as shown in Table 1.

Table 1 Relative distribution of individuals affected by Start Help, the 300 hours rule and the SA ceiling. (Source: Dahl et al. (2009).

	Receiving Start Help in 2006	Persons affected by the 300 hours rule	Persons affected by the SA ceiling in 2006
Immigrants	81	93	68
Natives	19	7	32
Total	100	100	100

Summarizing the main findings in the studies discussed in this section they fall in two groups, i.e. a number of studies covering fairly long periods of time before the major policy changes around the turn of the century and another number of studies, for obvious reasons with shorter observation periods, covering part of the years since the policy changes.

In the pre-2000 studies, some main findings are
- Overall negative fiscal impact from migration
- Take up of SA among immigrants much higher than corresponding to their share of the population
- Stronger cyclical sensitivity in SA take up for immigrants than for natives
- Big incentive challenges regarding "making work pay"
- Welfare dependence mostly a duration effect

In the post-2000 studies after the main changes in immigration and integration policies, some main findings are
- Job training in private firms, language courses and wage subsidy programs have a significant positive impact on job finding
- Specific policy changes with focus on reducing economic incentives for welfare take up are mostly found to have positive, but small, effects on employment and at the same time they result in considerable reduction of income for those covered by the changes who do not find a job
- Until now, many of these findings are more or less preliminary as the period over which post-policy change data are available still is fairly short

6. Development in welfare dependence since 2000

In this section we summarize a number of indicators of benefit dependence for the years since the turn of the century. First we present two different measures of annual benefit dependence. Next, we focus on one of these measures illustrating the profile in welfare dependence for all non-western immigrants and for a number of specific countries of origin. Then we go on to look at the profile over time in the average expenditures in the main welfare programs per individual, benchmarking against natives. And finally, the section presents some results from probit analyses of the probability of receiving SA in 2001, respectively in 2007.

We have looked into two simple measures of welfare dependence. The first, used in this section is called SBS and is defined as the ratio between the sum of UI, SA and Sickness Benefits and the individual annual gross income. The other measure called RBS is based on the socalled coherent social statistics and is measured on an individual level as the ratio between the sum of the annual number of days on UI, SA and Sickness Benefits and 365. We focus as mentioned on SBS but look briefly into the question of correlation between the two measures.

All individuals 18 – 59 years old are allocated into four different intervals of SBS, i.e. 0 – 0,1, with no or very low receipt of benefits, two intermediate intervals 0,1 – 0,5 and 0,5 – 0,8 and an interval 0,8 – 1 containing individuals fully or nearly fully provided for by one or more welfare programs. An overview of the change between 2001 and 2007 for the whole group of non-western immigrants is presented in Figure 8, illustrating a clear improvement regarding welfare dependence between 2001 and 2007[5].

Figure 8. Benefit ratio intervals. Non-western immigrants, 2001 and 2007.

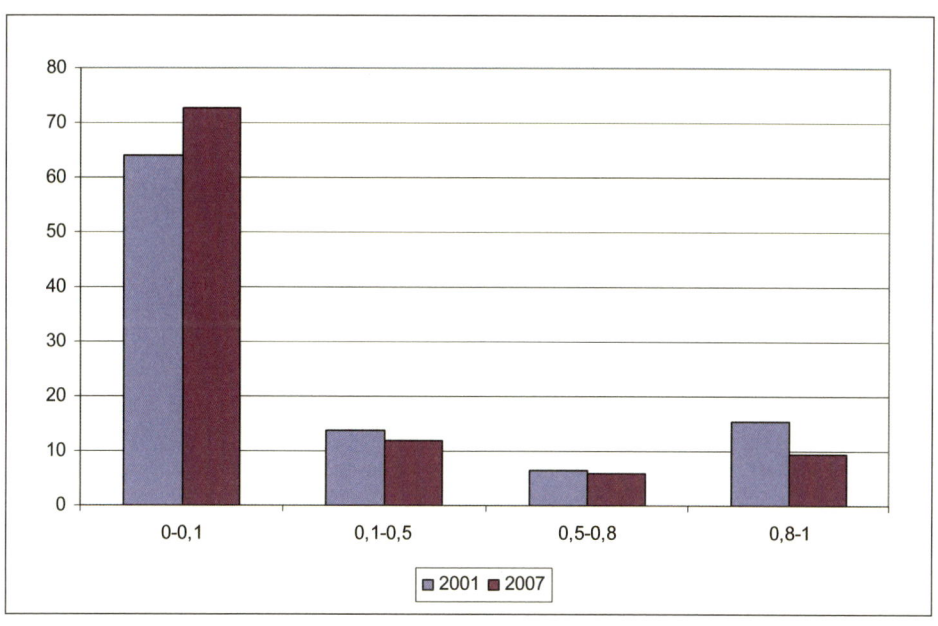

---

5 Comparable data for 2008 when unemployment was at the lowest level for many years are not yet available.

In Table 2 we illustrate the difference between 8 countries of origin and the distribution on intervals of SBS in 2001 and 2007.

Table 2. Benefit ratio intervals. Non-western immigrants, 8 countries of origin. 2001 and 2007.

		Benefit ratio			
Country	Year	0 – 0,1	0,1 – 0,5	0,5 – 0,8	0,8 - 1
Turkey	2001	58,0	19,2	9,2	13,6
	2007	65,6	15,9	8,1	10,5
Iraq	2001	58,9	11,1	6,3	23,7
	2007	59,5	14,5	8,2	17,7
Bosnia-Hercegovina	2001	65,4	13,8	5,3	15,5
	2007	76,7	10,5	4,8	8,0
Lebanon	2001	46,7	12,8	8,3	32,2
	2007	59,5	13,5	8,9	18,1
Iran	2001	66,3	11,9	6,4	15,4
	2007	77,2	9,6	5,1	8,2
Ex- Yugoslavia	2001	67,6	13,4	6,2	12,8
	2007	69,3	11,7	6,3	12,6
Pakistan	2001	62,3	14,3	7,2	16,1
	2007	68,7	12,2	6,9	12,3
Somalia	2001	41,0	14,9	9,6	34,5
	2007	50,6	21,0	10,6	17,8

In 2007 the highest level in the 0 – 0,1 interval is found for Iran and Bosnia with 75 – 80 per cent of the 18 – 59 years old in this interval. Looking at the absolute change in percentage points for this interval we find the highest value for people from Lebanon with an increase of nearly 13 percentage points. The highest share in the other extreme interval 0,8 – 1 is found in both years for immigrants coming from Iraq, Lebanon and Somalia. At the same time, however, we see a big decrease in this interval for these countries, especially so for people from Lebanon and Somalia. A final point is the finding of about the same standard deviation in both years for the 0 – 0,1 interval while the standard deviation falls to half the 2001 level for the shares in the high dependence interval 0,8 – 1, reflecting an inverse relationship between the initial level and the improvement measured by the decline in the share of immigrants in this interval.

In Figures 9 and 10 we illustrate the year to year variation in the average annual benefit ratios, first in Figure 9 for the three main guest worker countries along with people from Bosnia arriving as refugees in the mid- 1990s, and next in Figure 10 for four countries with immigrants coming as refugees and later as tied movers for family re-unification.

Figure 9. Annual benefit ratios (SBS), 2001 – 2007.

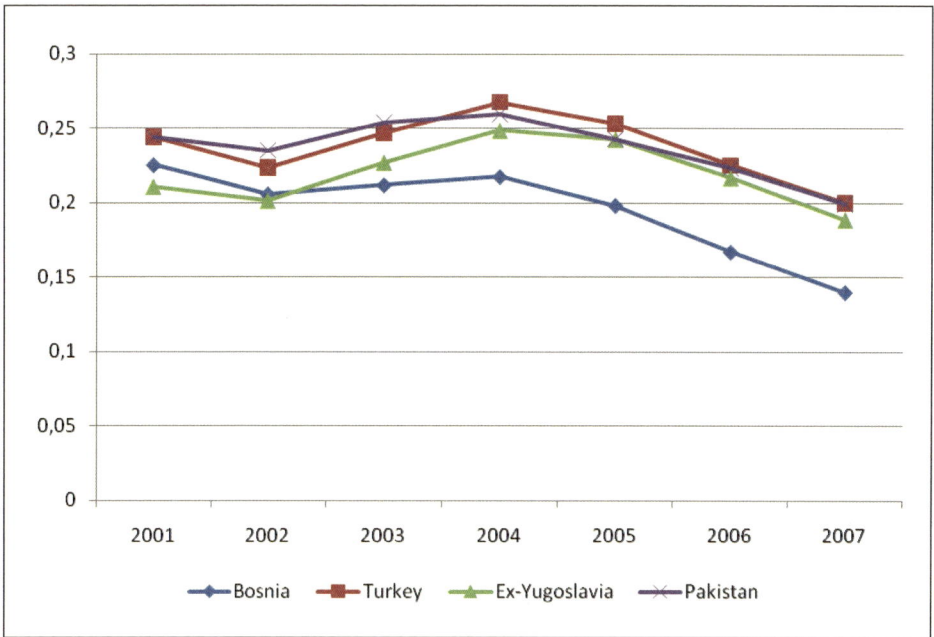

Figure 10. Annual benefit ratios (SBS), 2001 – 2007.

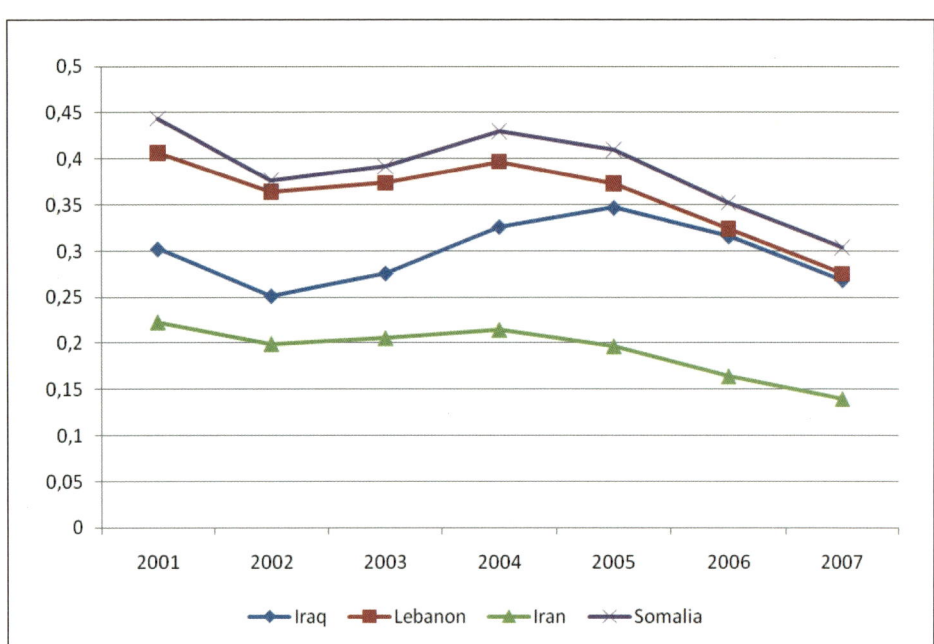

As mentioned we have also tried another welfare dependence indicator, RBS described above. As shown in the cross tabulation in Table 3 for 2007, the correlation is high between the two measures, especially so for the two "extreme" intervals 0 – 0,1 and 0,8 – 1.

Table 3. Distribution in 2007 on the alternative measures of welfare dependence SBS and RBS. Non-western immigrants, 18 – 59 years.

		SBS			
		0<=SBS<0,1	0,1<=SBS<0,5	0,5<=SBS<0,8	0,8<SBS<=1
RBS	0<=RBS<0,1	129948	2097	420	629
	0,1<=RBS<0,5	8413	11828	1077	1413
	0,5<=RBS<0,8	1562	4987	4853	1149
	0,8<RBS<=1	3869	4528	5189	15410

Another set of indicators of welfare dependence is presented in Table 4 showing for each of the years 2001 – 2007 the average expenditures per person in the labor force on UI, SA and Sickness Benefits for non-western immigrants benchmarked against natives. Except for Sickness Benefits the strong cyclical improvement since 2004 shows up for both immigrants and natives.

Table 4. Average expenditures on UI, SA and Sickness benefits. Non-western immigrants and natives, 18 – 59 years old, in the labour force. DKK. 2001 – 2007.

	2001	2002	2003	2004	2005	2006	2007
	Average amount, UI						
Non-Western	10.097	9.229	11.508	11.916	10.708	8.475	6.686
Natives	5.004	5.190	6.648	6.613	5.873	4.430	3.045
	Average amount SA						
Non-Western	16.289	14.415	14.746	16.291	15.918	13.628	11.154
Natives	1.916	1.983	2.146	2.450	2.410	2.152	1.936
	Average amount Sickness benefits						
Non-Western	2.742	2.555	3.500	3.672	3.631	3.899	4.475
Natives	1.755	1.721	2.478	2.692	2.655	2.799	3.116

In Figures 11 and 12 we show the ratios for UI and SA relative to natives for all non-western immigrants and for immigrants from four selected countries, i.e. Turkey and Pakistan as "old" guest worker nations and Iraq and Bosnia-Hercegovina initially dominated by refugees. Figure 11 has to be interpreted with some care. It appears as surprising that relative UI expenditures increase for immigrants as the relative unemployment goes down, cf. Figure 7. The explanation is institutional, i.e. as participation and employment goes up for immigrants a greater share becomes eligible to UI instead of SA in case of unemployment.

Figure 11. Relative expenditures on UI benefits. Average amounts for individuals in the labor force relative to natives.

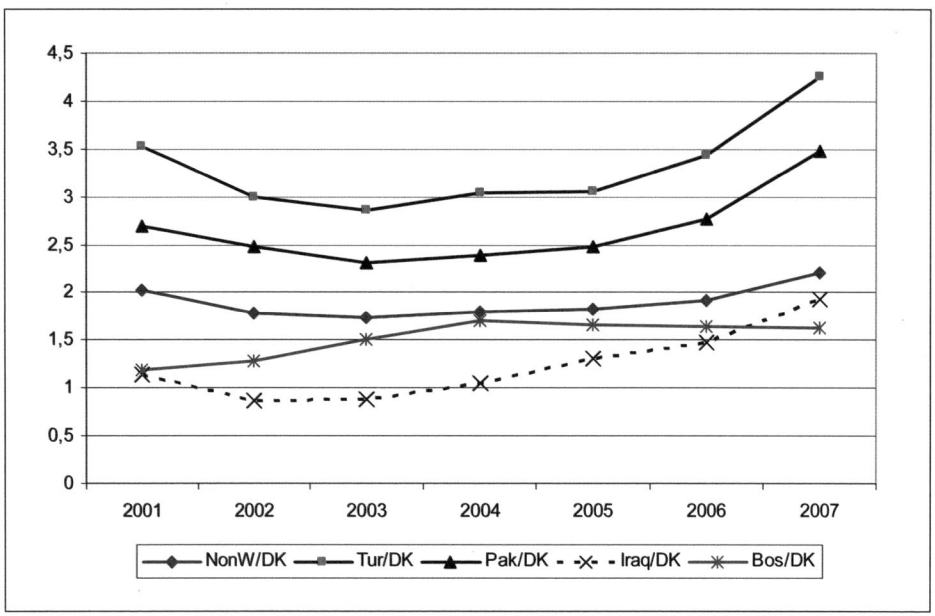

This explanation is illustrated in Figure 12 showing how relative average SA expenditures goes down for non-western immigrants relative to natives and especially so, among the included countries, for immigrants from Bosnia - Hercegovina. Adding average UI and SA we find a reduction of 28 per cent for natives and 32,3 per cent for immigrants where the big difference is average SA going down with 32 per cent for immigrants while it is constant (+1 per cent) for natives.

Figure 12. Relative expenditures on SA benefits. Average amounts for individuals in the labor force relative to natives.

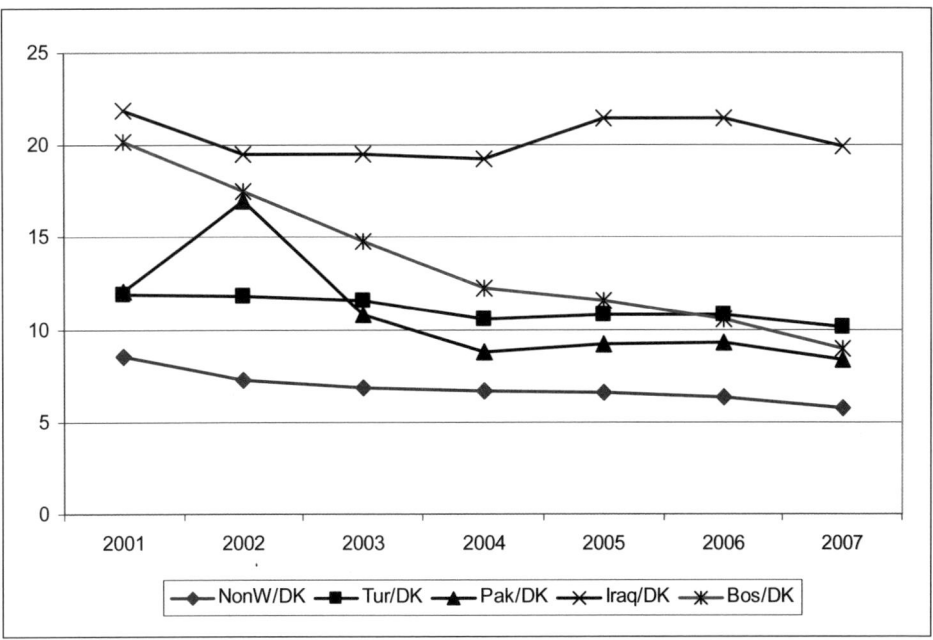

Finally, we present in Tables 5 and 6 the results from a probit analysis of the probability of receiving SA in 2001, respectively 2007 separately for all 18 – 59 years old non-western immigrants and natives. For 2001 we find clear differences in the impact from age. The excluded group is the 18 – 24 years old and for the immigrants we find a higher and increasing probability for ages 25 to 59. This is in complete contrast to the profile in age coefficients for natives where the probability peaks for the 25 – 29 years old and decreases with age. Women have a significantly higher probability for both groups. The variable civil status_0 is a dummy set at 1 for immigrants married to another non-western immigrant and at 1 for natives married to another native. Civil status_1 is set at 1 for a non-western immigrant married to a native and for natives married to a non-western immigrant. Marriage across the ethnic groups has a strong impact towards lower probability for receiving SA. Having one or more children 0 – 6 years old increases the probability of receiving SA while the impact from having older children is opposite between the two groups, most probably reflecting the different impact from age. Education has the expected sign. YSM, years since immigration has a highly significant impact pointing to assimilation out of welfare for the 18 – 59 years old.

Finally, we find significantly positive coefficients to the included countries of origin (India is the excluded country), as expected with the highest value of the coefficients for individuals from Iraq, Lebanon and Somalia. We find the same structure in the impact from the explanatory variables in 2007 as in 2001.

Table 5. Probit analysis of receipt of SA. Non-western immigrants and natives, 2001.

	Non-western immigrants			Natives		
	Coefficient	Std. Error	z value	Coefficient	Std. Error	z value
Age 25-29	0.0774	0.0153	5.07	0.0403	0.0049	8.24
Age 30-39	0.1254	0.0134	9.34	-0.0592	0.0044	-13.40
Age 40-49	0.2406	0.0150	16,07	-0.2874	0.0047	-61.29
Age 50-59	0.3066	0,0189	16,19	-0.9436	0.0057	-164.3
Gender	0.1527	0.0086	17.78	0.0793	0.0030	26.18
Civil status_0	-0.0863	0.0106	-8.14	-0.0296	0.0148	-2.01
Civil status_1	-0.8038	0.0177	-45.45	-0.5712	0.0035	-162.43
Child 0-6	0.2047	0.0057	36.07	0.1342	0.0027	48.83
Child 7-17	0.0691	0.0044	15.71	-0.0291	0.0024	-12.25
Education	-0.0445	0.0017	-26.53	-0.1871	0.0009	-205.5
YSM	-0.0394	0.0008	-48.79			
Turkey	0.4251	0.0548	7.75			
Iraq	1.1715	0.0559	20.94			
Bosnia-Herc	0.5920	0.0552	10.72			
Lebanon	1.1863	0.0558	21.25			
Iran	0.7425	0.0561	13.23			
Ex-Yugo	0.8970	0.1223	7.33			
Pakistan	0.4352	0.0566	7.69			
Somalia	1.3761	0.0569	24.20			
Other	0.5274	0.0539	9.78			
const	-0.7964	0.0600	-13.27	0.5834	0.0106	55.03
No. of obs.	116.713			2.792.288		
Pseudo R^2	0.1267			0.1394		

Table 6. Probit analysis of receipt of SA. Non-western immigrants and natives, 2007.

	Non-western immigrants			Natives		
	Coefficient	Std. Error	Z value	Coefficient	Std. Error	z value
Age 25-29	0.1564	0.0167	9.35	0.1077	0.0058	18.67
Age 30-39	0.2529	0.0140	18.01	-0.0106	0.0050	-2.12
Age 40-49	0.4083	0.0145	28.22	-0.1793	0.0050	-35.58
Age 50-59	0.4430	0.0169	26.22	-0.7787	0.0059	-132.69
Gender	0.1583	0.0083	19.14	0.1380	0.0034	40.66
Civil status_0	-0.2791	0.0102	-27.24	-0.2647	0.0177	-14.92
Civil status_1	-0.9248	0.0187	-49.37	-0.5713	0.0040	-143.79
Child 0-6	0.2457	0.0058	42.48	0.1409	0.0032	44.38
Child 7-17	0.1191	0.0041	29.17	-0.0618	0.0026	-23.77
Education	-0.0698	0.0016	-42.66	-0.2263	0.0011	-211.91
YSM	-0.0172	0.0007	-26.16			
Turkey	0.3902	0.0590	6.61			
Iraq	1.0417	0.0592	17.60			
Bosnia-Herc	0.3990	0.0597	6.68			
Lebanon	1.0773	0.0597	18.06			
Iran	0.6543	0.0605	10.81			
Ex-Yugo	1.0130	0.0752	13.47			
Pakistan	0.4491	0.0608	7.39			
Somalia	1.2260	0.0605	20.26			
Other	0.4935	0.0581	8.49			
Const.	-1.072	0.0634	-16.90	0.8162	0.0119	68.44
No. of obs.	148.885			2.608.492		
Pseudo R^2	0.1191			0.1613		

7. Conclusions

The extent of welfare dependence among immigrants and the answer to the question whether immigrants assimilate out of or into welfare benefits is the outcome of a highly complex interaction of many factors. There is big variation over time in the inflow of immigrants, there are changes over time in the composition of the inflow on job migrants, tied movers and refugees. Further, the cyclical situation at the time of entry and during the first years in a new country, qualifications from the home country, immigration and integration policies along with available welfare programs interact in ways making it difficult to disentangle the effects from the individual factors.

The focus has been on non-western immigrants as immigrants from western countries typically arrive to a job or an education and thus are much less relevant in discussions of welfare dependence. This is even more pronounced regarding immigrants from other EU countries as they have both higher employment rates and lower unemployment rates than immigrants from other Western countries. In contrast to immigration from western countries, non-western immigration has until the most recent years been unrelated to cyclical factors in the Danish economy.

Only from 1999 has a more explicit immigration policy been established with main emphasis on labor market integration. Since the mid-1990s labor market integration appears as quite succesfull. Participation rates have increased strongly, although the gap is still impressive relative to natives. Employment rates have also increased strongly, especially among younger immigrants since the turn of the century and unemployment has fallen sharply. Preliminary data indicates that non-western immigrants so far have been less affected by the crisis beginning in 2008 than natives. During the 2 years from February 2008 to February 2010, the number of people receiving unemployment insurance benefits has increased with 106 per cent for natives but only with 72 per cent for non-Western immigrants. Regarding Social Assistance, it is even more remarkable that the number of natives receiving SA has gone up with 35 per cent while it went down with 4 per cent for non-Western immigrants.

Traditionally, the Danish welfare state has been classified as belonging to the Scandinavian or universalistic type with equal eligibility to benefit programs for individuals with legal residence. Focus in the present paper is on non-permanent benefit programs. In this area there has been a number of policy changes with the purpose of restricting the amount and duration of benefit programs used mostly by immigrants. The explicit purpose is to influence incentives, making work more attractive but a side effect is a drop in income for those who do not get a job.

7. Conclusions

Existing Danish studies of welfare dependence among immigrants follow two approaches. One approach consists of aggregate studies of the impact from immigration on expenditures and revenues in the public sector. The other approach is micro oriented analyzing take-up and duration of specific welfare programs. Among the main findings is the obvious importance of getting entry to the labor market which is clearly associated with the macroeconomic situation both at entry and in the first years in the new country. Secondly, all available studies show a very big variation between countries of origin. Overall, results show assimilation out of welfare during the first 20 years of residence followed by assimilation into the permanent welfare programs for early retirement and Old Age Pension. Recent studies of the impact from active instruments to improve the chances for job finding conclude that efficient and early language training and wage subsidies to entry jobs in private firms are effective.

Studies of the policy changes focusing on restricting the amounts and duration of Social Assistance show until now an impact as intended on employment. The impact is however fairly small and the side effect until now has ben a drop in income for those in the affected groups who did not get a job.

For the most recent years, measures of welfare dependence among non-western immigrants point to a clear improvement in this area since 2001. Also here we find big differences in welfare dependence between different countries of origin, but with a clear pattern of strong improvement since 2001 for countries initially having the highest levels of welfare dependence. Among the individual programs we find the biggest decline in expenditures on Social Assistance to immigrants.

It is obviously of great importance that these improvements in recent years are not rolled back because of the current crisis. Preliminary data seems as mentioned above to indicate that non-western immigrants so far are less affected by the employment crisis than natives.

References

Bach, H. and B. Larsen. 2008. *300 – timers reglen. Betydningen af 300 – timers reglen for gifte kontanthjælpsmodtagere. (The 300 – hours rule. The importance of the 300 – hours rule for married recipients of social assistance)*. SFI Report 08:17. Copenhagen.

Barrett, A. and Y. McCarthy. 2008. *Immigrants and welfare programs: exploring the interaction between immigrants characteristics, immigrant welfare dependence and welfare policy.* IZA DP No. 3494.

Blume, K. and M. Verner. 2007. Welfare dependency among Danish immigrants. *European Journal of Political Economy,* 23, 453-471.

Borjas, G. J. (1999): "Immigration and Welfare Magnets" *Journal of Labor Economics,* Vol. 17, No. 4, pp. 607-637.

Clausen, J., H. Hummelgaard, L. Husted, K.B. Jensen and M. Rosholm. 2006. *Effekten af introduktionsprogrammets arbejdsmarkedsrettede indsats. (The effect of the labor market part of the introduction program.* (In Danish, with English summary)). AKF. Copenhagen.

Clausen, J., E. Heinesen, H. Hummelgaard, L. Husted, and M. Rosholm. 2009. The Effect of Integration Policies on the Time until Regular Employment of Newly Arrived Immigrants: Evidence from Denmark. *Labour Economics, 16,4: 409 – 417.*

Dahl, S., J. Quitzau and J. Vilhelmsen. 2009. *Hver 7. indvandrer lever i fattigdom (One out of 7 immigrants live in poverty).* AE Rådet. Copenhagen.

Danish Employers Association. 2006. *Vandringer og integration.* (*International Mobility and Integration).* Copenhagen.

Deding, M.C. and V. Jakobsen. 2008. *Employment among immigrant women and men in Denmark – The role of attitudes.* The Danish National Centre for Social Research. Working Paper 2008:8.

Economic Council. 2007. *Dansk økonomi. Efterår 2007. (Danish Economy. Autumn 2007).* Copenhagen.

Graversen, B.K. and K. Tinggaard. 2005. *Loft over ydelsen. Evaluering af loftet over ydelsen til kontanthjælpsmodtagere. (Ceiling to Benefits. An Evaluation of the Ceiling to Benefits for Recipients of social assistance).* SFI. Report 05:04. Copenhagen.

Hansen, F.K. and H. Hansen. 2004. *Starthjælp og introduktionsydelse – hvordan virker ydelserne? (Start Help and Introduction Benefits – Which impacts do the benefits have?)* CASA. Copenhagen.

Huynh, D.T., M.K. Schultz-Nielsen and T. Tranæs. 2007. *Employment Effects of Reducing Welfare to Refugees.* Rockwool Foundation Research Unit, Study Paper No. 15.

Huynh, D.T., M.L.S. Nielsen and T. Tranæs. (2010). The Employment Effects upon Arrival of Reducing Welfare to Refugees. Ch. 1 in M.L.S. Nielsen *Essays in Migration and Fertility.* Ph.d dissertation 2010:1. Aarhus School of Business. Aarhus University.

Ministry of Employment. 2005. *Afrapportering fra arbejdsgruppen om indsamling af oplysninger om virkning af introduktionsydelse på starthjælpsniveau/starthjælp. (Report from the Working Group on the Effects of the introduction of Start Help.* Copenhagen.

Nannestad, P. 2004. Immigration as a challenge to the Danish welfare state? *European Journal of Political Economy,* vol. 20, 755-767.

Nannestad, P. 2007. Immigration and welfare states: A survey of 15 years of research. *European Journal of Political Economy*, vol. 23, 512-532.

Nielsen, M.L.S. 2001. *The integration of non-Western immigrants in a Scandinavian labour market: The Danish experience.* The Rockwool Foundation Research Unit. Study no. 7. Copenhagen.

Nielsen, N-K. 2002. Overførselsindkomster til indvandrere. (Cash benefits to immigrants). Ch. 5 in G.V. Mogensen and P.C. Mathiessen (eds.) *Indvandrerne og arbejdsmarkedet. Mødet med det danske velfærdssamfund. (The immigrants and the labour market. Meeting the Danish welfare state). Spektrum. Copenhagen.*

Pedersen, P.J., M. Pytlikova and N. Smith. 2008. Selection and network effects – Migration into OECD countries 1990 – 2000. *European Economic Review,* vol. 52, 7: 1160 – 1186.

Pedersen, S. 2000. Overførselsindkomster til indvandrerne. (Cash benefits to immigrants). Ch. 5 in G. V. Mogensen and P.C. Matthiessen (eds.) *Integration i*

Danmark omkring årtusindskiftet. Indvandrernes møde med arbejdsmarkedet og velfærdssamfundet.(Integration in Denmark around the turn of the millennium. The meeting of the immigrants with the labour market and the welfare state). Aarhus Universitetsforlag.

Rasmussen, M. 2004. *Economic incentives and individuals' choice between welfare programs and work in Denmark.* The Danish National Centre for Social Research. Working Paper 2008:8.

Rosdahl, A. 2006. *Integration på arbejdsmarkedet af ikke-vestlige indvandrere og efterkommere. (Labour market integration of non-western immigrants and descendants)* The Danish National Centre for Social Research. Working Paper 2008:8.

Rosholm; M. and R.M. Vejlin. 2007. *Reducing Income Transfers to Refugee Immigrants: Does Starthelp Help You Start?.* IZA Discussion Paper No. 2720.

Wadensjö, E. and H. Orrje. 2002. *Immigration and the public sector in Denmark.* The Rockwool Foundation Research Unit. Aarhus University Press.